HAND TOOLS FOR THE HOME WORKSHOP

D1096509

HAND TOOLS FOR THE HOME WORKSHOP

DAVID X. MANNERS

THEODORE AUDEL & CO.

a division of

HOWARD W. SAMS & CO., INC.

4300 West 62nd Street

Indianapolis, Indiana 46268

Contents

1

Handsaws

Despite the inroads power sawing has made, handsaws still have an important place in any tool collection. They form a large group of more than a dozen varieties.

Leading the group in usefulness are the *crosscut saw* and the *ripsaw*. They come 16" to 26" in length and with hardwood or plastic handles. The 26" length is standard. The 16" size is good where storage space is limited, as in a toolbox or kitchen drawer. Blades may be of conventional steel, stainless steel, or steel coated to prevent rust, provide easier action, and keep blades gum-free.

If you expect to use your crosscut and ripsaw with any regularity and intensity, get good ones. Poor steel dulls fast, and may even buckle. Some better saws are taper-ground— they are thinner on the back edge than on the cutting edge—for easier action and to prevent binding. Others have a blade crown. Sight along the teeth and you will see they rise to a slight crest at the blade's center. This crown helps speed cutting.

The more teeth (or points) a saw has per inch, the finer its cut and the slower its action. Most crosscut saws have 8, 10, or 12 points per inch. The 8-pointer, the most popular, is an all-purpose saw. The 10-point and 12-point saws are for finishing work. Ripsaws are standard at 5½ points per inch.

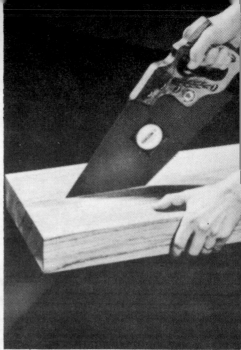

Crosscut saw (left) is used for cutting across the grain of wood. Ripsaw is used for cutting with the grain of wood. This one is Teflon coated to prevent binding.

Because ripping, or cutting with the grain, is essentially a chiseling action, the teeth of a ripsaw are filed at the tip, like chisels, and each tooth is lined up directly behind the one in front of it. Crosscut-saw teeth are filed like knives, so that each tooth is a sharp bevel that shears its way. The teeth have "set." This means they point outward, each alternate one in the other direction.

Miter saws are designed for use with a miter box in cutting angles. A good saw and miter box arrangement can be relied on to cut miters more accurately than a power saw. A miter saw may be 24″ to 30″ long and has a thick steel reinforcing spine along its length. Because it is for fine finishing work, it has 11 points per inch, and unlike other saws that are held

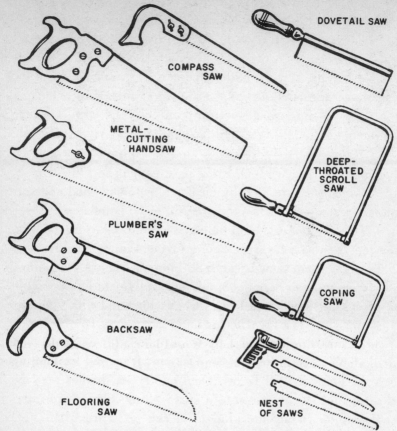

Assortment of handsaws for various jobs.

at an angle, it is held horizontally and cuts with its teeth parallel to the work.

Backsaws are similar to miter saws but shorter (10" to 14"). A backsaw's stiff blade and small teeth adapt it to making precision cuts and close-fitting joints.

Dovetail saws, as the name implies, are for cutting dovetail joints, which they do with extreme precision. A dovetail saw is also useful for cutting tenons and in making models, toys, and other small-scale, finely detailed projects. Typically, it is 10" long and has 15 points per inch.

Plumber's saws are for the kind of wood-cutting a

plumber usually does—flooring, joists, studs and the like, where nails may be a hazard. Hitting an occasional nail doesn't ruin a plumber's saw. It is 16″ long and has 8 points. One type has its handle attached with a wing nut. You can reverse the position of the handle so it's out of the way on awkward cuts.

Flooring saws make their own starting hole. The back edge of the blade tip is curved and has teeth to make a starting slit.

Metal cutters. These are 18″ to 24″ long and may have 13 or 15 points. They're for cutting light-gauge sheet metal.

Cable saws are used by electricians to cut wood and soft metals. Usually 12″ long, they have 8 or 15 points.

Docking saws get their name from their use around docks, but they're also a favorite among farmers, mine workers, etc. They are rugged, skew-backed, 30″ long, and have 4½ points.

Compass saws are the hand-held equivalent of a portable electric saber saw. Usually 12″ to 14″ long and with 9 points, a compass saw is a favorite for making cutouts. To make such a cutout in the middle of a plywood panel, for example, you drill a hole, then insert the compass saw. It is used for making cutouts for electrical boxes. On some types, blades may be reversed for sawing down to a surface, and blades are interchangeable. Among the kinds you can get are carbon steel blades for metal cutting, spring-tempered steel for plywood, and several varieties for woodcutting.

Keyhole saws are smaller versions of the compass saw. Usually they're 10″ long and have 10 points.

Nest-of-saws. This is a handy arrangement, with three saws fitting on one handle. There is almost always a keyhole (10″) and a compass (14″) blade, plus either a nail blade (14″), a plumber's blade (18″), or a pruning blade (16″). Similar are combination saw kits. Usually, they consist of a metal handle and an interchangeable rough-cut blade and a finishing-cut blade.

Coping saws are for making irregular cuts or curves in light stock or softwoods. Their blades have 15 or 16 points.

The usual throat opening permits a 4½″ to 5″ cut, but "deep throat" models may give a 6½″ cut. Some coping saws have an adjustable blade angle. Lowest-cost versions have a one-piece frame made of steel rod.

Pruning saws, for trimming trees and vines, come with either curved or straight blades. The latter may have either a single or double edge. The double-edged saws usually have fine peg teeth on one edge for small branches, and twin-pointed teeth on the other edge for large branches. For trimming high branches, there are pruners that have a socket into which fit standard clothes-pole or garden-tool handles. A straight pruner 20″ long is popular for cutting firewood.

Bow saws have a tubular steel frame shaped like a bow. The blade of a bow saw, usually ¾″ wide, has large teeth designed especially for cutting firewood.

Butcher saws are available in special small size for kitchen use in cutting meat. Typically, they are 14″ long and have 13 points to the inch.

Hacksaws. Every shop needs one of these. Get a good one for you'll be using it for cutting pipe, tubing, BX cable, sheet metal, plastics, asbestos board, and many other uncooperative materials. A hacksaw consists of two parts—a frame and a blade. You will use the same frame to accommodate several different types of blades.

Hacksaw is used for cutting metal.

The frame may be flat or tubular. Some are adjustable to accommodate either a 10″ or a 12″ blade. Some take a 12″ blade only. A tubular frame may store extra blades within it.

13

Frames differ in throat size, but the distance between blade and frame usually will be 2¾″ to 3½″. Some frames permit horizontal as well as vertical mounting of blades.

The most important feature of a frame is that it be rigid, and that it hold blades tight and in accurate alignment. You don't want blades to twist or wobble when the going gets rough, and with a hacksaw it frequently does.

For working in tight quarters, you won't use a regular frame. You'll use special hacksaw blade holders. One can get in a hole no larger than ⅝″. Another, called a "stab saw," needs only enough clearance for the blade to get at the work. It will hold an entire blade or the broken end of a blade.

A hacksaw blade may be of standard steel, molybdenum, or tungsten. It may be flexible or hard-tempered. Flexible blades help reduce breakage. All-hard blades are recommended only when work can be firmly positioned and when cuts are straight. Sometimes only the teeth are hard-tempered and the back is flexible. Standard steel blades, flexible or all-hard, are recommended for nonferrous metals and low-carbon steel.

Hacksaw blade holder, called a stab saw, permits cutting flush with a surface or in close quarters where a frame would be blocked.

Molybdenum blades are for high-speed sawing. They are extra rugged and can be used for fast sawing under adverse conditions. Tungsten blades command a premium price and are used only for such special jobs as cutting stainless steel, certain bronze materials, etc.

All blade varieties are available in coarse, medium, fine, and very fine. These have 14, 18, 24, and 32 teeth respectively. Choose a blade with enough teeth so that in use at least three teeth will be in contact with the work. Otherwise teeth may straddle the work and "shell" off.

Coarse blades are for cutting soft metals, like aluminum, brass, bronze, and copper, in stock $\frac{7}{32}''$ thick or better. The 18-tooth medium blade is best for all-round use. It will handle almost any job acceptably and it can eliminate the nuisance of constantly switching blades to get the one recommended for the exact job.

The 24-tooth blade is especially designed for cross-sections $\frac{1}{16}''$ to $\frac{1}{4}''$, items such as pipe, angles, and small rods.

The 32-tooth blade is especially designed for cutting stock up to $\frac{1}{16}''$, such as sheet metal, light tubing, and BX cable.

Blades with 14 and 18 teeth per inch have teeth set in "raker" pattern. Teeth in 24 and 32 blades have a "wavy" set. Armed with this knowledge you can tell at a glance if a blade has 14–18 or 24–32 teeth.

2 | Hammers / Hatchets / Mallets

A shop cannot have too many nail hammers. On many projects it's convenient to have hammers in several locations. It saves carrying one hammer back and forth, and cuts down time wasted in looking for a one-and-only.

Nail hammers are essentially of two types. One is the *claw hammer*, with a curved claw designed for pulling nails. The other is a *ripping hammer*. Its claw is straight, making it easier to get under boards and pry them free or apart. Most hammers come in three weights. The weight is that of the hammer head. The 13-ounce hammer is for light work or for use by someone who can't handle a heavier hammer. The 16-ounce weight is the one most people like. It can tackle almost anything. For driving 16- and 20-ounce spikes, however, the 20-ounce hammer has an advantage. But you won't want to use it ordinarily. On small stuff, it's too heavy for accurate control. Sometimes a 20-ounce hammer is referred to as size No. 1, a 16-ounce as size 1½, and a 13-ounce as size 2.

All-steel hammers are favored by many shopmen. These have tubular or solid handles that are permanently locked to the head. There never is any danger of the head coming loose. Usually they have a perforated, neoprene-rubber grip. This

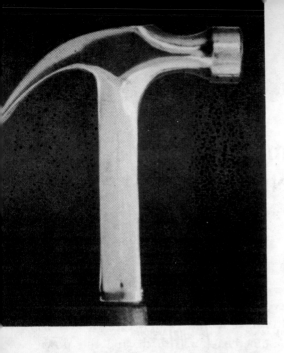

Claw hammer is designed for pulling nails.

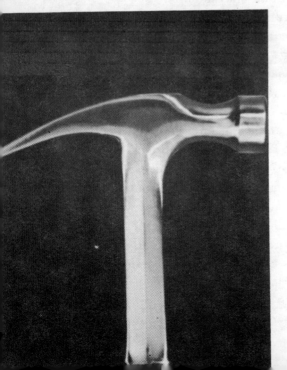

Ripping hammer has straight claw for prying.

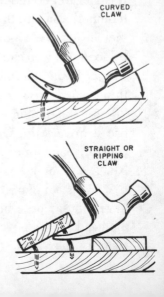

CURVED CLAW

STRAIGHT OR RIPPING CLAW

has a more comfortable feel than a wood handle and is less tiring. It absorbs shock better.

Don't waste money on a bargain hammer. Its head, in most cases, is of cast metal. If you yank too hard on a nail, it will lose a claw. Further, it is seldom balanced properly. It doesn't have a comfortable, authoritative feel. It is only good for driving nails crooked. Cast-iron hammers usually have a painted black finish.

A good hammer has a forged head. Its nailing face is chamfered (beveled) so that the edge won't chip. The striking face has a slight crown to match the arc of a normal striking swing and to provide a square, true blow. The crown also permits driving a nail flush with the surface without damaging the area around the head. A plain-faced hammer leaves marks when nails are driven flush.

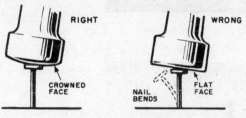

Crowned hammer face matches the arc of the swing and hits a fair blow. Nail doesn't bend. Flat hammer face hits nail at an angle and bends it.

A flying chip from a hammer face may cause injury. Stanley especially tempers its hammer face rims so that they have a lower degree of hardness and won't chip. A rim-tempered hammer may still have a hard-tempered face.

The kind of handle a hammer has affects its balance and the way it feels in your grasp. Rest a hammer across a narrow board and you will find that one with a wood handle balances close to the head. A hammer with a solid steel handle will balance farther back. Those with fiberglass or tubular steel handles balance somewhere in between. It all depends on the weight of the handle as compared with the weight of the head.

Ball peen hammer is used for metalworking.

Ball peen hammer. For working on automotive equipment and machinery a ball peen hammer is the natural choice. Instead of a claw this hammer has a rounded end called a peen. The peen is used mostly for riveting. The three most popular sizes are 6 ounce for light work, 12 ounce for average duty, and 16 ounce for heavy work.

Stone hammer. Handy for concrete and masonry work, and for use with chisels and star drills, is a drilling or stone hammer. These come in 2-, 3- and 4-pound weights. Choice depends on individual preference.

Bricklayer's hammer. If you lay brick or block you will want a bricklayer's hammer. These are available both with hickory and tubular steel handles.

Drilling hammer is used with a star drill for boring concrete. The drill is revolved a partial turn after each blow.

Bricklayer's hammer has a chisel edge at its face and rear. Either one can split a brick, but the face is especially good for nibbling away irregularities.

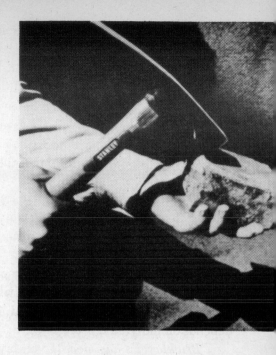

Sledge. For breaking rocks, demolition work, splitting logs, and other heavy hammering jobs, a sledge is a must. Select a sledge you can swing with relative ease. This will probably be a 12-pound weight. It takes extraordinary strength to swing a 20-pound sledge effectively.

Soft hammer. This tool is used on all the materials that might be damaged by ordinary steel hammers. In many cases a pounding block with a regular hammer is a good substitute. This spreads the blow and protects the surface. Among softies, plastic-tip hammers are a favorite. One variety has one tip of vinyl, which won't mar aluminum, wood, or polished surfaces, the other tip of amber plastic for use on iron, steel, etc. Amber plastic tips are replaceable. .

Mallet. This wooden hammer is used to drive some wood-handled chisels and gouges. Chisels with tough plastic handles capped by steel take the blows of a conventional hammer and are the best choice for the shop.

Hatchet. To an old-time carpenter, a hatchet was one of the most important tools. In rough carpentry, when a board was to be trimmed, he used a hatchet. It takes off wood faster and easier than a plane or a saw. When a shim, shingle, or board had to be split to size, the hatchet got the call. You will find the hatchet useful for all these purposes and more. Use it wherever a chisel's more accurate cutting is not desired or required. The flat side of a hatchet can be used as a hammering tool.

The most useful hatchet for the home shop is the half hatchet. Its blade is extra thin. Half hatchets come with either a single or double bevel. The single bevel is best for hewing to a line. When hewing to a line, a series of cuts are made against the grain to the depth of the required cut. The board is then reversed and the notched wood removed to the depth of the cuts. For deeper cutting, the process may be repeated. Chopping should be done with the grain whenever possible. The single bevel can be used only with the right hand. The double bevel is an all-purpose hatchet.

3 | Planes

A plane is a tool for making wood smooth and flat. It is used for paring a little off the edge of an oversized board, and for taking the sharp edges off a board or panel, an operation known as chamfering.

Out of the wide assortment of planes available, three types figure importantly in the home workshop—the block, the jack, and the jointer plane.

The *block plane* is the smallest variety. Typically about 7″ long, it is held in one hand when in use. This small size makes it easy to handle, and it's the plane most men reach for when just a little has to be trimmed from a board or an edge taken off. It's a champ at end-grain.

The *jack plane* comes in several sizes, but typically it will be 14″ long and have a blade 2″ wide. It's an all-round, all-purpose plane. The smooth plane is similar to the jack plane except that it is smaller and lighter. Typically it's 8″ or 9″ long and has a 1¾″ blade.

The *jointer plane* is the largest variety. Typically 20″ to 24″ long, it's for producing true flat edges on long boards so they fit perfectly together. A prime use around the house would be for planing a door edge. A fore plane is like a jointer except that it's shorter—usually about 18″ long. Remember—

Useful planes for the home workshop (from left): rabbet plane, a specialized type for cutting rabbets; smooth plane, a light-duty plane similar to the jack plane but shorter; rough or scrub plane, with a rounded cutting edge for heavy stock removal; and jack plane, an all-purpose plane for truing boards of moderate length.

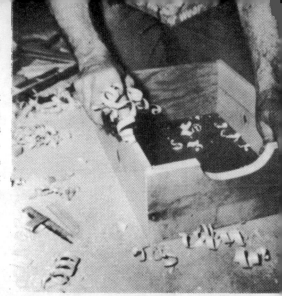

Block plane's blade is set at a lower angle than blade in other planes; thus it cuts faster and with less resistance. It will make an edge smooth but, as it is short, not necessarily true.

Jointer plane is designed for truing up long edges, as on a homemade plank door. The longer the plane, the better it is for smoothing and truing a long span of lumber.

the longer a plane, the more readily it bridges low spots, cuts the high ones, and produces the kind of smooth results you want.

Special planes are made for doing specialized jobs such as rabbeting, routing, grooving, etc. Most of these jobs can be done by power tools easier, faster, and more accurately, so they have little application in the home shop. A saw and jointer can do many of the jobs that in other years would have been done with a plane.

PLANE ANATOMY.   The plane iron or blade is what does the cutting. The depth of cut depends on how far it projects through the mouth on the bottom of the plane. This is controlled by a knurled knob. For best results, the iron should project a bare fraction. For an even cut, the blade must be set straight. Set at an angle, it will cut deeper on one side than on the other. There is a lever for making lateral adjustments.

On jack, smooth, fore, and jointer planes there are double plane irons. The top one serves to stiffen the plane iron and curl up the shavings. The distance of the plane-iron cap from the edge of the cutting blade controls the thickness of shavings. After making any adjustment, tighten the cap so it fits very tight. Otherwise, there may be danger of shavings getting between the cap and the blade. The iron cap isn't needed on a block plane because there is no problem of clogging the mouth. A block plane is used only in cutting end-grain, which produces a powder, or in fine shaving.

Some planes have grooved bottoms. The purpose is to make them slide smoothly and with less friction.

If a plane won't cut, you're trying to make too thick a cut, or the blade is dull. It should be razor sharp. If your cut is rough, it usually means you're cutting against the grain. For a smooth cut, you must go *with* the grain. Don't use a plane on painted or varnished wood. It won't do a good job and you'll dull the blade.

In making a rough cut, slant the plane across the board as you push it. The best technique for a finish cut is to put pressure on the front of the plane when starting the cut and on the rear when finishing it. This prevents breaking end corners. When planing end-grain, avoid breaking corners by planing from each end to the middle. You can use a jack or smooth plane on end-grain, but the block plane is preferred.

Store planes so they are protected from rust and damage to the cutting edge. An enclosed cabinet is best. Stable the planes on a rack made of two ½″ wood strips. The forward strip acts as a stop. The rear strip elevates the plane so it doesn't rest on its blade. For wall mounting, make a shelf with an area routed out into which the plane's blade can project.

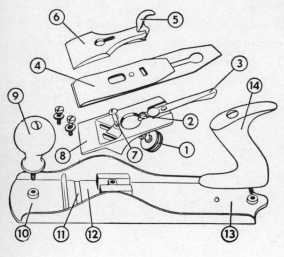

PARTS OF A PLANE
1. Depth-adjustment nut
2. Y-lever
3. Lateral-adjustment lever
4. Double plane iron
5. Cap lever
6. Cap
7. Cap screw
8. Iron support
9. Knob
10. Toe
11. Mouth
12. Bottom
13. Heel
14. Handle

and reason. . . . With few exceptions that would chance to have
it found its way into the copy. The text ordinarily chosen
was not . . .

4

Chisels/Gouges/Punches/ Nail Sets

There are chisels made especially for cutting wood, metal, and masonry. With the exception that a cold chisel, which is designed for metalworking, can be used on masonry, chisels are not interchangeable. If you expect to work with all three materials, get chisels made for each one.

WOODWORKING CHISELS.   The kind of handle on a woodworking chisel determines the use for which it is intended. There are three kinds of handles found on the various chisels available to the woodworker.

For light work, the easy paring away of stock which can be done by hand pressure alone, or by the lightest blows of a mallet, you can use a *tang chisel*. The tang is the rattail end of a chisel, and it is enclosed in a handle of wood, plastic, or other material.

Some chisels have a socket on one end instead of a tang, and a handle of wood or other material fits into this socket. A *socket chisel* is designed for heavier duty than a tang chisel and to be struck with a mallet. The handle comes out rather easily and is replaceable.

The best type of chisel for the home shop, and a favorite

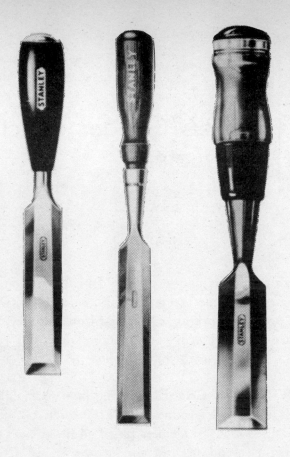

Three types of wood chisels (from left): tang chisel with handle enclosed in plastic; socket-type firmer chisel; heavy-duty chisel with steel cap and amber handle.

with carpenters, is the *heavy-duty chisel*. You can hit it with a steel hammer. The steel of this chisel extends up through the handle and forms a striking face. One type of heavy-duty, or everlasting, chisel is all steel. It has an hexagonal shank and a round head.

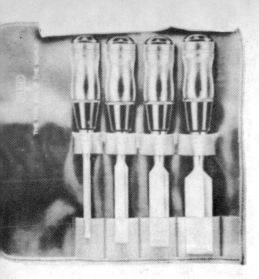

Set of butt chisels in ¼″, ½″, ¾″, and 1″ widths.

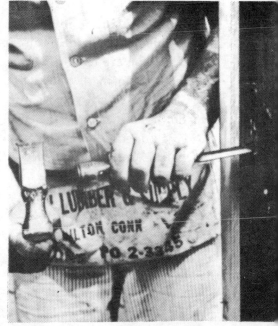

Butt chisel being used to cut mortise for hinge on a door.

There are other words you'll hear used to describe chisels. They relate to differences in the length and thickness of blades and their principal use. There are paring, firmer, butt, and mortise chisels. A pocket chisel is not one you carry around in your pocket. It is just another name for a mortise chisel.

Paring chisels, which are used without a hammer, usually have tang handles. The blade is short, light, and thin. The short blade makes it possible to maintain excellent control over the chisel and cutting angle when hand paring and carving.

Butt chisels get their name because they are primarily used for cutting the mortise when installing a butt hinge.

Firmer chisels have the longest blades, giving them a wide range of use. They usually have socket handles.

Chisels come in widths starting at ⅛″ and increasing by ⅛″ to 1″. After that, the progression is by ¼″, then jumps to 2″. The ¼″, ½″, ¾″, and 1″ sizes are best for average home needs.

Tips on using a chisel. Always keep both hands behind the edge of the blade. If it slips, you won't hurt yourself.

When you are hand-powering a chisel, supply the power with one hand, using the other to control the cut.

Chisels have a beveled cutting edge. Rough cut with the bevel down, finish cut with the bevel up.

To get a straight cut when the width of the cut is wider than the chisel, allow each succeeding cut to overlap the previous cut by about one-third.

When you're chiseling along an edge, work from the edge toward the center. If you work in the other direction, you may ruin the edge.

Take out the bulk of the wood with a saw, drill, or plane. Use the chisel for finishing purposes only. Don't rush. Take small cuts. A large cut risks splitting the work.

Observe the direction of the grain where it meets the edge.

Cut in the same direction for smooth results. To cut counter to the grain direction means an uncontrolled cut and rough results.

GOUGES. These are like chisels except that the cutting edge is trough-shaped instead of flat. There are three degrees of blade curvature: flat, medium, regular. Bevels may be on the concave side and such gouges are known as inside-ground. Outside-ground gouges have the bevel on the convex side. An outside-bevel gouge is used in the same way as a chisel with the bevel down. It's a rough-cutting tool. An inside-bevel gouge is used like a flat chisel with the bevel up. If held at a wide angle, it will dig in.

In making any cut, rock the blade slightly as it is advanced so that there is shearing action. In cutting grooves, to

Carving-tool set consists of bent chisel, U tool, skew bevel chisel, veining tool, bent gouge, and carborundum stone. Pocketknife is a useful addition.

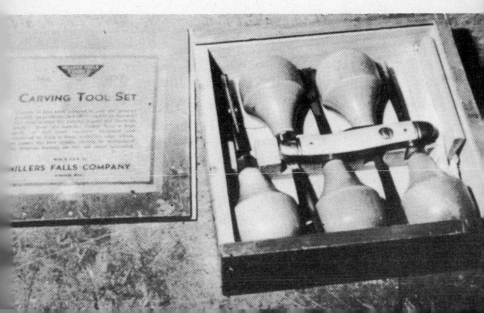

avoid damage to edges, start at the edge and work in. In cutting a groove, do it in several stages, getting deeper each time. Don't use the full edge of the gouge, only its inside arc.

Gouges are available with both straight and bent shanks. The bent shank is good for cutting long, shallow grooves. The handle being offset, it permits running the gouge almost parallel to the work.

You can get paring gouges and firmer gouges. Firmer gouges may be outside or inside ground. Paring gouges are inside ground only.

If your project includes carved moldings or panels, don't use carpenter's and cabinetmaker's chisels and gouges like those described. They can be used for rough cutting, but for fine detailing and sculpturing you need a set of carving tools.

A small carving-tool set includes a variety of gouges and a chisel or two. There are deep gouges called fluters and shallow ones called flats. Ones that cut a U-shaped gouge are called veiners. V-shaped gouges are called parting tools. Chisels may have a square cutting edge or an edge at an angle to the blade. There are spoon-bit chisels for digging into right corners and left corners, dog-leg chisels for situations where an offset is needed.

COLD CHISELS.   Essentially metal-cutting tools, cold chisels will cut wire, rods, and sheet metal. They will cut away a rusted nut or rivet that you can't reach with a hacksaw. A cold chisel will cut any metal softer than itself.

A cold chisel is classified by the shape of its point. Besides the classic flat cold chisel with its straight shank and a tip like a screwdriver, there are round-nosed chisels, for chipping rounded corners and cutting trough-shaped grooves; diamond-point chisels, for cutting V-grooves and square inside corners; and cape chisels, for cutting narrow grooves. There are also special "rivet shear" chisels, for rivet cutting.

Cold chisels for cutting metal (from left) : cape chisel, for cutting narrow grooves; diamond-point chisel, for cutting V-grooves and square inside corners; round-nosed chisel, for chipping rounded corners and cutting trough-shaped grooves.

Flat or plain cold chisels and diamond-point chisels are the ones most useful to the homeowner.

The smaller the chisel point, the greater its impact. That is why to cut off a large rivet head, a good mechanic will first cut a slice through the center of the rivet head with a cape chisel, then cut off the head with a flat chisel. The larger the chisel and the chisel point, the heavier the hammer you must use with it.

The size of a chisel is determined by its cut, stock, and length.

Safety with cold chisels. Wear goggles. Don't allow spectators within line of flying chips.

Always chip away from yourself.

Keep the chisel sharp. Use an emery wheel to maintain the point and keep the original angle. Note that the cutting edge of a flat chisel curves to a high point at the center. Keep a chisel cool as you grind by dipping it in water. If you don't, the chisel edge will lose its temper and become soft.

The cutting angle should be about 60 degrees, not much more or much less.

Smooth away any "mushrooming" on the hammering end.

Center punch being used to make a starting hole in metal so that drill won't slip.

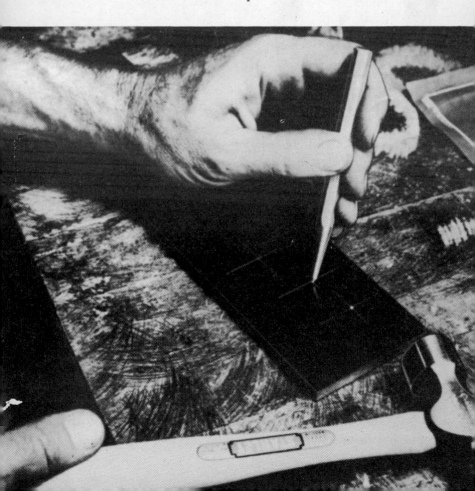

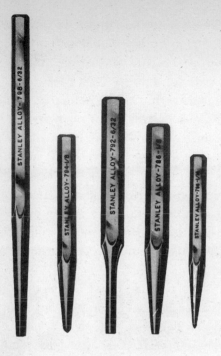

Set of punches for various purposes (from left): lineup punch, for aligning holes when fitting parts; center punches (2), for making a starting point when drilling metal; starter punch, for knocking rivet from hole after cutting off head; pin punch, for finishing the job.

One of those pieces might break off when you're hammering and hit someone in the eye.

When you are chipping work held in a vise, hammer toward the stationary jaw.

Use a diamond-point chisel to extract a broken-off bolt by drilling progressively larger holes into the stub until you have a hole large enough to pound in the chisel point. Then remove the bolt by turning the chisel with a wrench.

PUNCHES. There are starter, pin, line-up, center, and prick punches. Like chisels, the best way to buy them is in a set. If you can buy a good combination chisel and punch set, so much the better. A good set will include four chisels ranging in size from ¼″ to ¾″ and eight assorted punches. They are not expensive.

Use a starter punch to knock a rivet from a hole after its head has been cut off. You may need the long slender point of a pin punch to complete the job.

Use a lineup punch to line up holes on two parts being fitted together.

Use a center punch to make a starting point when drilling metal. It prevents the drill point from wandering. If you have a variable-speed drill and can start drilling at a very low speed, center punching may not be necessary, but it's still helpful. You can also use a center punch for marking the alignment of metal parts before you disassemble them. By aligning punch marks, there is no guesswork as to their exact positioning.

Prick punches differ from center punches in that they have a longer taper and a sharper point.

NAIL SETS.   Used to drive the heads of brads or finishing nails below the surface, nail sets can also be used for making starting holes for screws. Their size is determined by their point, which may be $\frac{1}{32}''$, $\frac{1}{16}''$, $\frac{3}{32}''$, $\frac{1}{8}''$.

Use a nail set whose point is a little smaller than the nail you are driving. If you use a larger nail set, you enlarge the hole unnecessarily.

Nail sets may be of round stock their entire length, or they may have square heads. The square head gives a slightly larger striking surface and keeps the tool from rolling when you drop it.

Set a nail head $\frac{1}{16}''$ or more below the surface to provide enough of a hole to fill. In some cases you may want to set flat-

Nail set is used to drive the heads of finishing nails below surface of wood or to make starting holes for screws.

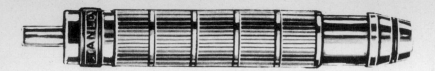

Self-centering punch centers screw holes accurately in countersunk hardware. It is also useful in setting finishing nails without marring wood.

head nails—on siding or clapboard for instance.

Use a nail set to prevent marring a surface by accidental hammer blows. Drive the nail close to, but not flush with, the surface. With a single sharp blow on the nail set, drive the nail below the surface. With repeated blows, you have less control. The cupped end of the nail set prevents its slipping off the head of the nail.

5 | Files / Rasps / Scrapers

FILES. There are more than 3,000 kinds, sizes, and cuts of files. Of these you will need about a half dozen for maintenance chores and projects. In both metalworking and woodworking, a file can accomplish things you can't do with other tools, so it pays to have a few of the most versatile ones in your workship.

The terminology used in naming files can be confusing to the novice, so before specifying what files you ought to acquire, it might help to explain the meaning of the most common terms.

The term "bastard" has nothing to do with a file's legitimacy but refers to the coarseness of its teeth. In describing coarseness, file makers use the progression dead-smooth, smooth, bastard, coarse, and rough. A bastard file, then, is one whose coarseness falls in the middle of the spectrum.

The terms "single-cut" and "double-cut" refer to the sharp ridges or teeth on the file surface. A single-cut file has sharp, parallel ridges running diagonally across its surface. A double-cut file has a second set of ridges crossing the first set at an angle, creating a crosshatch. Examine the crosshatch and you'll see it has created a large number of small, pointed teeth. The smoother a double-cut file is, the more and finer teeth it has.

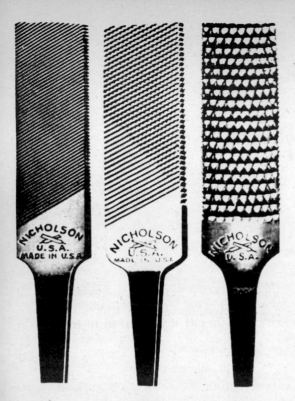

Three types of files (from left): single cut, double cut, rasp. Single- and double-cut files are used in metalworking, a rasp in woodworking.

A double-cut file cuts faster than a single-cut file, but it leaves a rough finish. A rasp has large, individual hooked teeth which slant toward the tip of the tool.

Aside from the differences in teeth, files may be round, triangular, square, flat, half-round, or mill. A mill file tapers in thickness and width in the third of its length near the tip. It gets its name from its original use in sharpening blades in sawmills.

Some files taper, other have a blunt shape. A tapered file is good for enlarging small openings. The blunt shape is good for filing inside corners. A half-round file is good on concave surfaces. A 6″ triangular file is good for filing notches, square holes, and for repairing damaged threads. A 6″ round file, often called a "rattail" file, is useful for enlarging holes and for filing small concave surfaces.

Sometimes one edge of a file is left smooth. This is called a "safe" file. When you are filing into a corner, the safe edge won't rough up the intersecting side. Mill files come with square or round edges or with one safe edge. You can grind the teeth off the side of a file and make your own safe edge.

Selecting files. Single-cut files are usually used for sharpening cutting edges, such as those on knives, shears, and saws. Use light pressure. Double-cut files are usually used where it is desired to remove metal fast and a rougher finish is acceptable. Use heavy pressure. Rasps cut very roughly and are used principally on wood, leather, and soft metals.

Triangular files are used for sharpening handsaws. They are usually single-cut. A slim-taper triangular file can be used for band-saw blades. Use a 7″ slim taper if the saw has four to six teeth per inch. Use a 6″ slim taper if it has seven to ten teeth per inch.

For all-round metalworking, a 10″ single-cut flat bastard file (top) is most favored. Triangular slim-taper file is used for sharpening saw blades.

Mill files are used on circular saws, planer knives, and lawn-mower blades. Use a round-edged mill file for sharpening circular-saw blades' rip and chisel teeth. Use a slim-taper triangular file for crosscut and combination-blade teeth.

Use rifflers, small files with curved ends used in wood

Two useful woodworking rasps: 8″ flat bastard rasp (top) and 8″ half-round bastard rasp.

carving, for irregular shapes and hard-to-get-at spots. Rifflers have a different shape at each end. Typically there is a rasp end for rough cutting, a file end for finishing.

Use a half-round cabinet file for shaping the cove on a table edge. Use a knife file for cleaning the V's in a scalloped edge. Use a round rasp or file for making flutings. Use a shoe rasp for filing slots or fitting tenons.

You'll probably use a 10″ mill and a 6″ triangular file most, so get these first. (The stated length of a file does not include its tapered end, or tang, which fits into the handle.) Also handy are a 10″ half-round double-cut bastard, a 10″ round bastard, a 6″ single-cut half-round, and a 6″ round. For working on wood you'll want a 10″ half-round rasp. If you do any wood carving you'll want a collection of rifflers, although these files come in handy for other work.

Using a file. The teeth of all files face toward the tip. That's why a file cuts on the forward stroke only and why pressure should be applied only on this stroke. On the return stroke, a file should be lifted slightly off the work. If you don't lift the file, you dull the teeth. On soft metals, however, allowing the file to drag lightly on the work as you pull it back tends to free material that might otherwise clog its teeth.

Chips can be cleared from the file teeth by occasionally rapping the tool sharply against wood. Really effective clean-

Rasp being used to bring a mortise-and-tenon joint to proper fit. It can also smooth end-grain cuts that have a rough finish.

ing of teeth is done by brushing with short, fine, wire bristles.

In rough filing, stroke across the work at about a 30-degree angle. For finish filing, keep strokes straight across. For best results, hold a file so it is exactly parallel to the work on its forward, cutting stroke. This is necessary to produce a flat cut rather than one that is rounded.

To produce a fine finish on a narrow surface, use a single-cut file and draw it sideways over the work, back and forth. It may produce a burred edge, but this can be quickly smoothed up.

If a file slides over hard metal, it's the wrong file for the

Files should never be thrown loosely into a drawer or piled on top of each other. Here are two types of racks for keeping files apart to protect cutting teeth from damage.

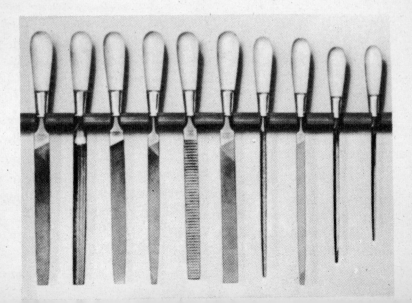

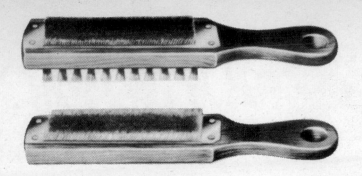

File brush at top combines card and brush and is used mostly for cleaning fine-cut files. File card below is for general file cleaning.

job. You are dulling the teeth, not cutting the metal.

A file works better after breaking it in. Use wears the teeth down so they are all the same height.

Handles. Every file needs a handle; it makes the file easier to use and also protects you from getting hurt by the sharp-pointed tang. To attach a handle firmly to a file, insert the tang in the hole of the handle; then, holding the handle with a firm grip, strike its butt end solidly against a wood surface until the tang is all the way in.

Care of files. Rust ruins files, so store them in a dry place. Don't throw them loosely in a drawer. In contact with one another, they become dull.

If a file card won't clean the teeth, try picking them clean with a sharp point. If sap or paint is the problem, soak the file in an appropriate solvent.

Don't oil files. It may prevent rusting, but it will also collect clogging dirt.

Handscraper is used by cabinetmakers to shape and
smooth rough-sawn stock.
Scraper is bowed slightly by
thumb pressure to provide
cutting action.

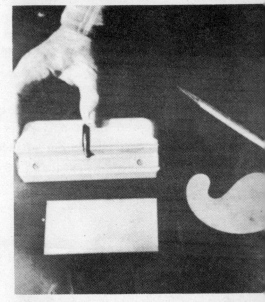

Rectangular and oval cabinet
scrapers with burnishing tool
used for applying an edge.

Surform tool has hundreds of
tiny, razor-sharp cutting
teeth, each with its own chip
opening to prevent clogging.
It shaves, shapes, and
smooths most materials.

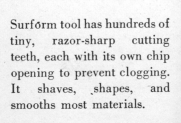

SCRAPERS. A cabinetmaker eliminates the need for much sanding by using a scraper. It takes off finer shavings than a plane. It will produce a smooth cut even against the grain and is a good tool for cleaning up along glue lines.

A cabinet scraper has a blade sharpened to a 45-degree angle, with a hooked edge which is turned over by "burnishing," using a special tool. The hook does the cutting. The blade is held in a frame that has two handles.

The scraper blade is adjusted by tightening a thumbscrew which springs the blade so its hook projects. In use, the tool is pushed away from you.

A hand scraper works like a cabinet scraper except that it has no frame. It is just a blade held in the hand. It may be rectangular or curved steel about $\frac{1}{16}''$ thick. It, too, requires a burnisher to create the burr or hook along its edge.

A rectangular blade may be held in one or both hands and pulled or pushed. On flat surfaces it can reduce sanding and finishing time. In fact, many expert woodworkers scrape instead of sand.

For curved surfaces there is a gooseneck-shaped scraper. It will handle jobs like scraping the inside of a wooden bowl which would be almost impossible otherwise.

A variety of fixed-handle pull scrapers is available for such jobs as removing paint, rust, etc. These have hook-shaped blades which may be single-edged and permanently attached to the handle, or double-edged so they can be reversed. The blade edges of some scrapers are straight, others serrated. The serrated type is especially good for digging into tough paint film, but it leaves groove marks.

6

Screwdrivers

Screws come in many sizes and varieties, and many sizes and varieties of screwdrivers are needed to fit them. A screwdriver that fits the slot properly does half the job of getting the screw in or out. The blade tip should fill the screw slot exactly, or at least three-quarters of it. If it fills less than that, it is likely to twist out of the slot and chew it up. If it's wider than the slot it will gouge the material into which you are driving.

How well a blade holds in a slot also depends on how good a driver you use, and how its tip is finished. Good blades are cross-ground. Inferior ones are ground lengthwise or made of pressed metal. Good tips are forged.

The most economical way to acquire a screwdriver collection is to buy a matched set. Matched drivers also make a more attractive display in the shop and toolbox. Finding the screwdriver you want is also easier when you have a single image of what to look for.

But a set is only the beginning on which to build the collection of drivers you'll need to satisfy every demand. To drive tiny screws with precision and ease you will need a set of midgets. For portability, you will want a kit with many blades that fit into a single handle. For awkward situations, you will want screw-launching drivers which have gripping sleeves to

Screwdriver should fit the slot of the screw to do the job properly. Standard blade at left it too wide for the screw, will damage the wood. Cabinet blade, right, is too narrow, will twist out and damage the slot.

hold the screw. You will want an offset driver for situations where you can't get in with anything else. Its lever action multiplies torque (twisting force) many times. Also good for multiplying torque is a bit brace. A variety of blades are available to fit it.

A standard screwdriver has a blade that fans out just back of the tip. This extra width is convenient for getting a grip on the blade with a wrench when extra leverage is needed. However, it prevents the tip from following a screw into its hole. You can't recess screws into deep holes in furniture, for example, with a standard blade. For this purpose, as well as for elec-

Types of screwdrivers and the screws they fit.

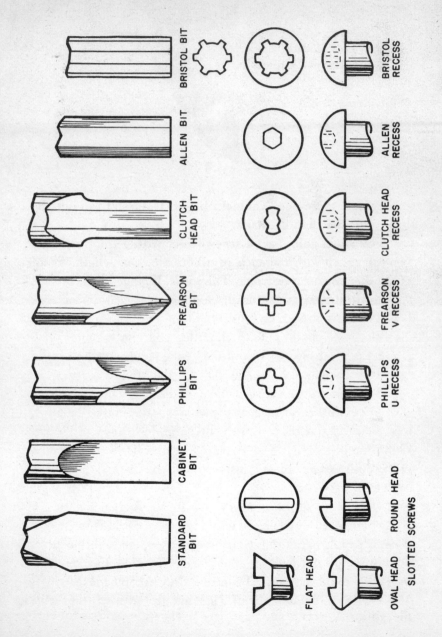

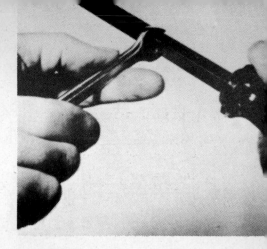

Square-shafted screwdriver is designed for use with a wrench to hold blade in slot and gain maximum torque.

tronic work, there is a "cabinet" blade. It doesn't fan out; its tip is no wider than its shank.

For tough going, get a screwdriver with a square shank. You can grip it with a wrench anywhere along its length. Avoid using pliers on a screwdriver. They will damage it.

A traditional rule is: never hammer on a screwdriver. But, as usual, there are exceptions. One type of screwdriver has a shaft that extends through the handle. You can hammer on it as much as you please. The blows strike steel, not the handle itself.

The best test of a screwdriver handle is how it feels in your grip. Most screwdrivers these days have plastic handles. Will those deep flutes cut into your palm on heavy use? Many plastic handles are covered by rubber grips. These cushion the hand, offer protection against electric shock, and may give extra turning power.

Old-timers say, use a pry bar for prying, not a screwdriver. Once a screwdriver shank is bent, it is difficult to restore. If prying breaks off a corner of the tip, the tool is useless. Blade tips are hardened to make them durable and keep the ends from rounding over. The harder they are, the more brittle. Reworking a broken blade may salvage it, but it will never be the same.

Usually the shank and blade (or tip) of a screwdriver are referred to as the blade. A screwdriver's size is the combined length of its blade and handle.

SPECIAL SCREWDRIVERS. Phillips screwdrivers fit screws with cross slots. Besides their attractive appearance, these screws have the advantage of preventing the blades from slipping out of the slot and gouging the work. One size of Phillips driver can handle a range of screws, but it may take pressure to seat the driver in the cross slot. Similar to the Phillips screwdriver is the Frearson bit, which fits screws whose cross slots are slightly concave.

Three other types of screw heads require special drivers: clutch head, Allen recess, and Bristol recess. The hex-shaped Allen screw may be removed either with an Allen wrench or an Allen-bladed screwdriver. The Bristol recess is shaped like a rounded six-pointed star. The clutch head recess is shaped, roughly, like an hourglass (or butterfly), or like a flat, blunt-tipped propeller.

A close cousin of the screwdriver is a "turnscrew." This is a screwdriver made especially for wood screws. Handles are eggshaped or oval rather than cylindrical, this giving them unexcelled twisting power. The upper blade is flattened to take a wrench.

For electrical work you may want to get an insulated electrician's screwdriver. This has a blade coated with resistant plastic to protect you against accidental shorts. A good insulated electrician's screwdriver will protect you up to 5,000 volts. Never use an ordinary screwdriver to check an electrical circuit where the amperage is high, as on standard house voltage. If an electrical current is strong enough to arc, it will damage the screwdriver blade. Spark plug current may be high in voltage but it is low in amperage. It may be safely tested with an ordinary screwdriver. Better are screwdrivers made especially for circuit testing. These have fully insulated handles and blades, making them completely safe. The handle lights up to indicate a hot wire or side.

If you work on radio or television receivers, you will have need for a driver made of a nonmetallic material. It is used for the lining of sensitive tuning gear, which cannot be done with a metal driver.

There are a variety of "reversible" screwdrivers. While you are using one blade, the other blade is concealed in the handle. For a different blade, you merely pull out the one you are using and reverse it. A good combination is one that pairs a Phillips with a regular blade. For working with small parts, there is a "mini" reversible with a pocket clip. It has a ⅛" regular bit on one end and a No. 1 Phillips bit on the other. It comes with a special protective pouch that fits in your pocket. One reversible set is three-way. Besides the reversible screwdriver, a ¼" nutdriver is built into the dome of the handle.

Screw-holding driver is essential in tight quarters. It grips screw firmly while starting and holds it as it is removed.

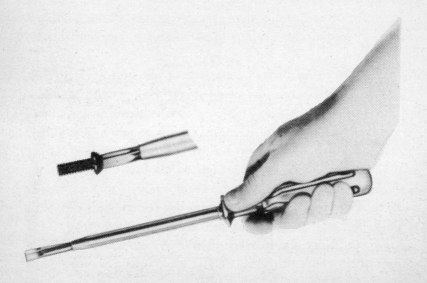

Another reversible set has a single cushion-grip handle and four double-ended blades.

There are many screwdriver novelties. You can buy magnetized screwdrivers which, as the name implies, will pick up and hold screws. A key-shaped screwdriver is available in the popular ¼″ width to fit your key chain.

Nutdriver bits in sizes from ³⁄₁₆″ to ½″ are commonly available. These can be used in screwdriver handles made for interchangeable bits and are especially effective in ratchet-type handles.

RATCHET SCREWDRIVERS. Spiral ratchet screwdrivers are time- and labor-savers. One push on the handle turns a screw almost three times. The direction of drive can be reversed, or it can be locked. It is then a rigid screwdriver. A quick-return spring in the handle permits one-hand operation. Some have three-way ratchet action without the spring-return.

Most ratchet drivers come with three screwdriver bits. For

Spiral ratchet screwdriver speeds up work and reduces effort. One push on the handle turns a screw three times.

some, you can get an accessory set that includes cabinet bits, drill points, and a countersink. There are offset ratchet screwdrivers for both slotted and Phillips head screws.

Oxwall distributes a pistol-grip ratchet screwdriver with an aluminum chuck. It comes in a kit with three blades. The pistol grip gives it 45 percent greater turning power. There is also a type of ratchet handle that has a brace which fits into it. Any of a number of screwdriver tips then fit into the collet at the end of the brace. The brace provides crank action and multiplies power.

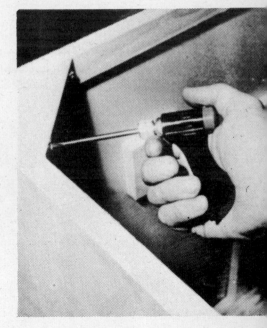

Pistol-grip ratchet driver with interchangeable blades is useful for light work. The pistol grip gives added turning power.

7 | Nutdrivers

On many jobs where hex nuts and screws are used, you'll need a nutdriver, a tool that resembles a screwdriver except that in place of a blade it has a socket that fits over the nut or the screw head.

Most nutdrivers fit only one size hex nut, but there are others that are self-adjusting to a variety of sizes. One manufacturer, Vaco, makes a nutdriver that automatically adjusts to sizes from ¼″ to 7/16″. It has multiple nesting hex sockets and when the driver is pushed down on the nut, the appropriate socket slips over it.

Stanley's Hex-a-Matic accommodates fifteen standard sizes of nuts and screws. These include five sizes of hex nuts from ¼″ to 7/16″, five sizes of hex-head screws from No. 8 to 5/16″. It will also fit all metric-sized fasteners up to 11 mm. It works by means of a six-fingered collet chuck which adjusts automatically to the required size and locks into position when the driver is pushed down.

Unlike tools with multiple, nesting hex sockets, the Hex-a-Matic has an infinite range of adjustment. It will fit and hold on even damaged nuts and screws. It is available as an attachment for Stanley's Yankee spiral ratchet screwdriver. Com-

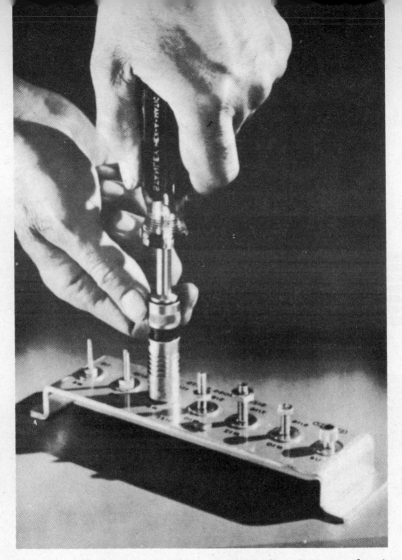

Hex-a-Matic nutdriver automatically adjusts to the size of nut or screw head. Disassembled collet chuck (below) shows six fingers that enable tool to fit any hex-head nut or screw within its range of capacity.

bined with the ratchet screwdriver, it has an extra-long reach, a valuable feature in getting at remote fasteners in large appliances or TV cabinets.

Extensions, commonly 5″ long, are available for many nutdrivers. A good kit to have is one with an interchangeable handle that accommodates hex bits, a variety of screwdriver bits, and a series of nutdriver bits. Vaco offers one kit with thirty blade styles and three handle styles, all interchangeable. You can get pouches with seven, fourteen, or thirty-six sections. This permits starting with a basic kit, and adding pieces later as you require them.

Four types of adjustable wrenches (from top): chain wrench; monkey wrench; heavy-duty pipe wrench; adjustable open-end wrench.

8

Wrenches

A bike, car, lawnmower, plumbing fixture, oil burner, air conditioner—you can't repair any of them without wrenches. Having the right kinds and knowing how to use them can save you time and heartburn.

There are five basic types of wrenches you need and should know about: adjustable, open end, box, socket, and pipe wrenches. This is also the probable order in which you will acquire them. Though all are made for nuts of one kind or another, each wrench has its own special merit and purpose.

ADJUSTABLE WRENCHES. The monkey wrench was the first of the adjustable variety. It has largely been superseded by wrenches that are lighter and handier. The simple adjustable wrench included in most automobile kits resembles the monkey wrench, but in scaled-down form. Obviously, its advantage is that it will fit nuts of many sizes. However, the automobile wrench can't be used unless there is easy accessibility and swing space.

Somewhat more maneuverable is the adjustable-end wrench. Because its jaws are set at a 22½-degree angle to the handle, it can get in places where the ordinary adjustable wrench cannot. By flipping it over, the grip is varied so that a new hold can be taken on a nut with only half a swing.

The limitation of an adjustable wrench is that it doesn't keep its adjustment and is likely to slip and chew up the nut. It also lacks durability. If you don't push it in the direction of the jaws you may break the lower one. If you don't keep the jaws snug on the work, you may break off the teeth in the adjusting mechanism. It is definitely not a wrench to break loose frozen nuts, or to snug nuts excessively tight.

A series of adjustable-end wrenches made by P&C overcomes the tendency of the ordinary adjustable-end wrench to lose its adjustment. By ingenious design, every adjustment clicks and holds.

In buying an adjustable wrench look for the word "forged" or "drop-forged" on the handle. Forged metal is stronger than cast metal. Drop-forged means that the metal was formed by being forced into a die under a drop hammer.

Wrench size indicates overall length. A 6″ wrench has a capacity up to ¾″. A 10″ size has a 1⅛″ capacity. You can buy a three-piece set, which includes the popular 6″, 8″, and 10″ sizes for less than you would pay individually. Adjustable-end sizes generally range from 4″ to 20″. The 20″ has a maximum opening of 2½″.

OPEN-END WRENCHES. The opening, not the length, determines the size of an open-end wrench. If the jaw opening at one end is ½″ and at the other ¹⁹⁄₃₂″, it is a ½″ by ¹⁹⁄₃₂″ wrench. The length of the wrench, however, determines its leverage, and manufacturers proportion length to opening in accordance with what they feel use demands. Wrench ends are usually at a 15-degree angle. Flopping the wrench permits continuous turning of a hex nut in a 30-degree swing.

A wrench end should fit the nut exactly, so you need a collection of them. A typical six-piece open-end set has wrenches with openings ranging from ⁵⁄₁₆″ to 1″. A set of ten wrenches with openings from ¼″ to 1⅛″ provides every size you are likely to need in the home. Sets usually come with kits in which they can be kept.

For tubing connections of oil burners, air conditioners, and refrigerators, a flare nut wrench is useful. It is a specialized kind of open-ender.

BOX WRENCHES.   These fit over a nut or bolt head and surround it completely. The "box" is a circle of twelve notches, so you may hear it called a twelve-point wrench.

Because the box construction is sturdier than open jaws, this wrench can be thinner, permitting you to get into tight

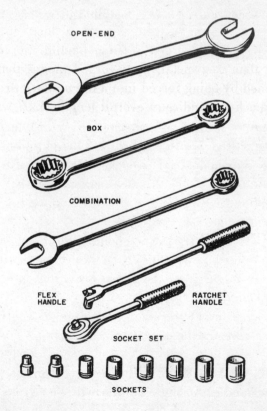

Four different kinds of fixed wrenches.

places with it. You can loosen or tighten a nut with a swing of only 15 degrees. In contrast, the open-end wrench requires 30 degrees, even when flopped. If not flopped, it takes 60 degrees.

Another advantage of the box wrench is that it is easier to keep on the nut. It can't slip like an open-end wrench. That's why it is a favorite for breaking loose tight nuts and getting the last quarter turn on a nut that is being snugged down.

In use, a box wrench must be lifted off the nut and repositioned for each added turn. That makes the open-end wrench just a little faster. For this reason some wrenches are made with a box at one end and an open-end at the other. The box can then be used for the tough jobs, and the open-end the rest of the time. Both ends in a combination wrench fit the same size nut.

As always, the longer the wrench handle, the greater the leverage. That is why a length of pipe is sometimes slipped over a wrench end. This makes it possible to apply a much greater torque, but unless done carefully it can result in a ruined wrench and/or work. The same caution or prohibition applies to striking a wrench with a hammer. There are, however, special heavy-duty industrial wrenches made for use with long extension handles. There are others, called "striking wrenches," that have a square striking surface for use with a sledge or hammer.

Skinned knuckles are a common problem when using wrenches. Some box wrenches have their handles tipped up at a 15-degree angle from the head, providing a clearance to spare your knuckles.

Box wrenches also come in ratcheting style. Turning over the wrench reverses the direction of the action.

SOCKET WRENCHES. The secret of this tool's success lies in its handle. A single handle will fit all the sockets in the set.

It may be a ratchet handle. This means that the socket

doesn't have to be raised off the nut at each swing. By flipping a little lever, the ratchet will either tighten or loosen a nut. By means of a "ratcheter," any nonratcheting handle can be made into a ratcheting tool.

With a hinged offset handle, you can swing the handle down at right angles to the socket and get tremendous leverage. When the nut has broken loose, the handle can be raised to a vertical position and turned between the fingers.

A sliding offset handle can be positioned so as to make up a T handle. Or it can be set to one side for increased leverage. It can be used in combination with an extension bar to get at hard-to-reach nuts.

A speed handle works like a brace. It makes short work of nut removal once the nut has been broken loose by use of the offset or ratchet handle.

In close quarters and awkward situations, a universal joint makes it possible to use the speed handle at any angle to the socket.

Handles for socket wrench sets come in four sizes, the size being determined by the square peg on the drive end of the handle. The sizes include $\frac{1}{4}''$ drive (or midget) for light-duty work, a $\frac{3}{8}''$ drive is for medium work, and $\frac{1}{2}''$, $\frac{3}{4}''$, and $1''$ for various jobs. The $\frac{1}{2}''$ drive is most popular for working on cars, and a fifteen-piece set will have sockets ranging from $\frac{7}{16}''$ to $1\frac{1}{4}''$. You can buy auxiliary handles and attachments later.

Also useful for the homeowner is the $\frac{1}{4}''$ drive set. At modest cost you can get a twelve-piece set including nine sockets to fit $\frac{3}{16}''$ to $\frac{1}{2}''$ nuts, with a flex handle, crossbar, and metal case.

A handy accessory for your drive handles are screwdriver sockets. These come for regular, Phillips head, and hollow head screws.

Torque-limiting handles are used in working on engines

and other equipment where tightening must be done according to specifications supplied by the manufacturer. Unless you are a car buff, they have limited application in the home shop.

Better-made sockets have thin walls for getting into tight places. They are chrome plated to resist rust.

PIPE WRENCHES. These are for turning and holding pipes, rods, and other things that do not have flat sides. The pipe wrench differs from the ordinary wrench in that it has teeth in its jaws. On other adjustable wrenches, the lower jaw moves. On the pipe wrench, it's the upper jaw.

The Stillson is the most familiar variety of pipe wrench. The toothed arm that moves its jaw up and down is loose within a retaining collar. This collar pivots on a rivet or shaft, which permits the upper jaw to have a rocking motion. When you pull on a Stillson, the hingelike action of the jaw closes it on the work. Relax your pull, and the biting jaw comes free.

Because of its teeth, a pipe wrench should not be used on any finish you don't want to mar. Wrapping a cloth around a chrome pipe helps some, but it is no positive insurance against damage.

You need a pair of pipe wrenches for most jobs. One wrench holds, the other turns. They don't have to be the same size. A 10" Stillson will take pipe up to 1". An 18-incher takes pipe up to 2". They make a good pair.

Similar to the Stillson is the "heavy duty" pipe wrench. It differs from the Stillson in that its collar doesn't pivot. The toothed-jaw arm is loose within its collar and this is what permits its action. It sells for almost twice as much as the Stillson variety.

One kind of pipe wrench has a hex jaw. It is made especially to provide a nonslip grip on hex and square nuts. Its smooth jaws won't harm plated finishes, so plumbers use it for a nonslip grip on sink and tub drain nuts, etc. It is also available in an offset model with the jaws at an angle to the handle.

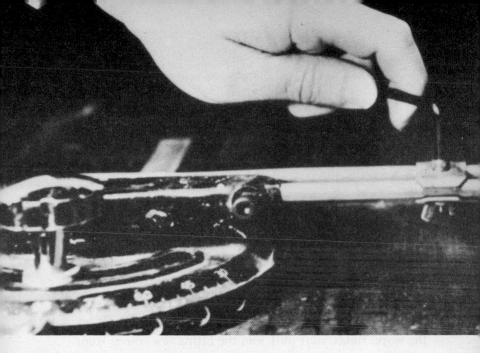

Allen, or key, wrenches are useful in the shop for adjusting headless setscrews, as on the miter gauge of this table saw. They are available in a set, with sizes to fit every size setscrew (below).

Some straight and offset pipe wrenches come with aluminum handles. These are about 40 percent lighter than standard wrenches.

A chain pipe wrench uses a chain instead of toothed jaws to get its grip. It is especially good for working in tight places. It fits pipe, conduit, or irregularly shaped material. It has a ratcheting action and a big capacity. A chain pipe wrench with a 12″ handle and a 15″ chain can handle pipe from ¼″ to 4″ in diameter.

Operating on a similar principle, but using a strap instead of a chain, the strap wrench has the advantage of not chewing up the work. A 12″ strap wrench, typically, has a break strength of 3500 pounds, and has from ⅛″ to 2″ capacity.

SPECIAL WRENCHES. Indispensable in the installation or removal of faucets and in getting at hard-to-reach nuts, the basin wrench with its foot-long handle and self-adjusting jaws is a valuable tool to have in your shop. Its jaw flips over for reversing direction.

Allen or setscrew wrenches are for headless setscrews. A typical complete set comes in a plastic pouch and includes every size you'll ever want. Because some of the most useful sizes invariably get lost or disappear, you might consider getting a set in which the various keys are inseparable. One kind has them opening up like the blades in a pocket knife. You can also get Allen heads for your socket-wrench set.

To the British, every wrench is a "spanner." In countries where a wrench is a wrench, the name spanner is reserved for devices with hooks or pins. These fit into holes or notches on the nut to be turned. Most of them come in service kits furnished with appliances or other equipment.

9

Pliers / Snips / Nippers

PLIERS. Wrenches supply their own grip; with pliers you supply the grip. Your grip on the handles of a pair of pliers is multiplied many times by mechanical advantage into a powerful force. An 8-pound pressure on the handles can become a 300-pound pressure on the object between the jaws. Considering that most jaws measure about $\frac{5}{16}''$ by $\frac{5}{16}''$, this is about $2\frac{1}{2}$ tons per square inch.

A well-equipped shop may have a dozen or more different kinds and sizes of pliers. Some grip, some cut and grip, while some only cut.

Slip-joint pliers. Of the six kinds of pliers every shop should have, No. 1 on the list is a pair of slip-joint pliers. You'll use them for everything from pulling out a cotter pin to tightening the Sunday roast on the barbecue spit. The pivot rivet joining these pliers slips into two, sometimes three positions, varying the jaw opening from a slit to over an inch. Plier size is measured by length. Common sizes are 5", 6", 8", and 10", with the 6" and 8" sizes the most popular.

Good slip-joint pliers have joints that work easily, but not sloppily. Their shear-type wire cutter won't work if the joint is sloppy. The wire will slip between the cutters, which

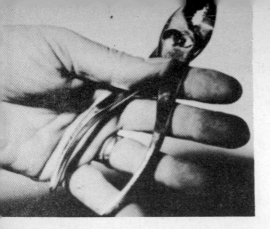

Slip-joint pliers adjust to two or three positions, varying the jaw opening from a slit to over an inch. For shear-type wire cutter to work effectively, joint must work smoothly but not loosely.

will chew it instead of cutting it. One type of slip-joint pliers has a special hard-steel side cutter. Another has thin jaws, extending like a long, slim nose. This slim nose will reach into tight places. Still another, called the "multi-plier," which has a four-position slip-joint, provides compound leverage that multiplies applied pressure ten times. Some slip-joint pliers have double-curved jaws that can grip 3/16″ stock or 1″ pipe with equal force.

Engineer's pliers. A very useful type of pliers has jaws which open 1½″ or more with the jaws remaining parallel. They are commonly called engineer's or pump pliers. Typically, they have five channel adjustments, but they may have as many as eleven. They are especially good for plumbing jobs.

Engineer's pliers have great gripping power. Pair at left is best for gripping pipes and other round objects. Pair at center is designed for gripping flat-sided objects like bolts. Smooth-jawed pliers, right, won't damage plated finish on plumbing fixtures.

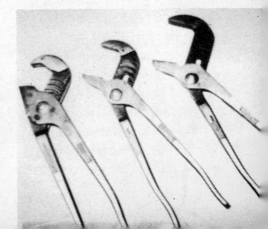

One type has smooth jaws that will not mar chrome fittings. You'll use them for taking off traps or disassembling faucets. Unlike ordinary pliers, engineer's pliers can handle nuts without mangling them or your hand.

Battery pliers. These pliers, with their long handles and tiny jaws, have great gripping power. A 7½″ pair has only ½″ capacity, but where titan-like force is required, they are the ones you'll use. Their upper jaw is angled and toothed, perfect for wrapping around a recalcitrant hex nut.

Parrot-nose plier wrenches combine the action of pliers and a pipe wrench. They exert a powerful grip and are ideal for pipe and tubing.

Locking-plier wrenches. For loosening rusted nuts and studs, use locking-plier wrenches. They are a clamping tool and vise, as well as pliers, and have many workshop applications. Their powerful jaws, which may be either flat or curved, are quickly adjusted to fit the work; then, with a squeeze, they lock tight. No more than a finger touch is needed to release them. "Vise Grip" and "Grip-Lock" are two popular trade names.

Parallel-jaw pliers. These pliers fit snugly on nuts, and because of their compound-leverage design have unexcelled gripping power. This leverage also helps their wire-cutting action. They'll cut a 10-penny nail. Wire can be fed through an opening between the handles so that a straight, head-on grip

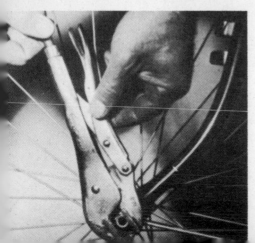

Locking-plier wrench does many of the jobs commonly assigned an adjustable open-end wrench, but it is far less delicate. It has teeth that bite, and because it seldom slips, doesn't mangle the work.

on the wire is possible. This is useful in making splices or in winding springs around a form. The pliers are available with either toothed or smooth jaws. The smooth ones are kind to highly polished finishes and are effective in breaking away narrow cuts of glass.

Five kinds of pliers are especially useful for electrical work.

Lineman's pliers have a fixed pivot which gives them cutting action far superior to that of slip-joint pliers. Their cutting edges run half the length of their jaws. They can cut soft metals, such as copper, brass, and aluminum, but are damaged by hard steel. The flat surfaces on the jaw end are suited for gripping wire and flat metal.

Button's pattern pliers are a special variety of electrical pliers with a curved gripping section in the jaws. Wire cutters are on the outside of the jaws. Their action is a shearing one, similar to that in slip-joint pliers, but because of the tightly-fixed pivot they do a much better job.

Needlenose pliers have a very thin nose. They're good for getting into places with restricted clearance. The thin nose is especially useful in bending and shaping wire, as at terminals. For getting around obstructions, you can get needlenoses with the nose bent at a 79-degree angle. Needlenoses are useful in retrieving nuts or other small parts which fall into inaccessible places.

Diagonal cutting pliers are indispensable in electrical work. They excel at cutting, and their thin, narrow nose can reach into tight spots to nip wires and perform other operations. Their diagonal slant makes it possible to flush-cut without the handles getting in the way. Diagonal pliers are good for spreading cotter pins and for removing them.

Wire strippers are essential in most electrical work. As strippers, they cut the insulation but not the wire. An adjustable stop equips them to handle wire of various sizes, typically from 12 to 26 gauge.

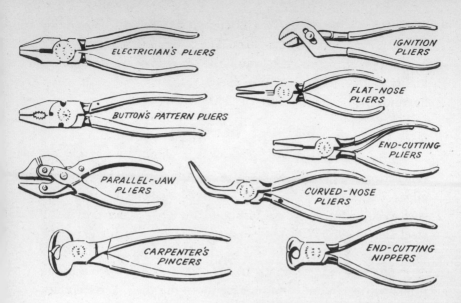

ELECTRICIAN'S PLIERS

IGNITION PLIERS

BUTTON'S PATTERN PLIERS

FLAT-NOSE PLIERS

PARALLEL-JAW PLIERS

END-CUTTING PLIERS

CURVED-NOSE PLIERS

CARPENTER'S PINCERS

END-CUTTING NIPPERS

Pliers and cutters which are useful in the shop.

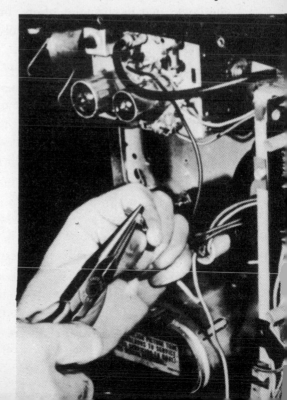

Needlenose pliers can cut wire to length and form the ends in the proper shape to fit a terminal screw.

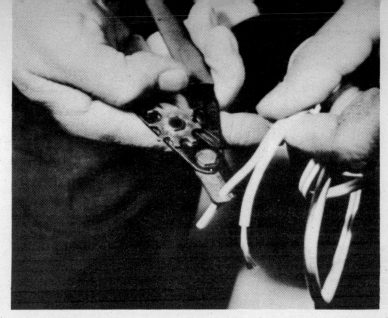

Wirestrippers are adjustable to every size wire commonly found around the house. They neatly cut the insulation, but not a hair of the wire.

Another tool that can be used for cutting and stripping wire is one that can also be used for crimping solderless terminals to wire and for slicing bolts. Typically, there are separate holes in which wire from 10 to 22 gauge can be inserted for stripping. There are also holes for inserting six sizes of bolts. The bolts can be sliced neatly with no burrs remaining to be filed.

SNIPS.   Shears used for cutting thin sheet metal are called snips. Aviation snips are unexcelled for cutting thin sheets of aluminum, copper, or galvanized steel. They have compound-lever action so that cutting is effortless. If you don't ruin them by attempting to cut heavy metal, they will last forever. Never exert more than hand pressure on them. These compound-power snips are of three varieties: one type cuts to the left, another to the right, and the third cuts right or left.

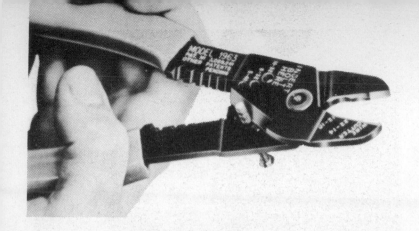

This tool cuts and strips wire, crimps solderless terminals to wire, and slices six sizes of bolts without leaving burrs.

Straight-cut snips demand more muscle power. One way to get it is to insert the lower handle in a special slot in the workbench top. You can then put all your weight on the upper handle for tough cutting jobs. A 12″ size is a good choice.

When cutting with snips, insert the sheet metal all the way into the jaws. Cutting with a "full run" of the blade means a smoother cut. To avoid overrunning a cut, use the tip ends of the snips for complete control.

Wiss manufactures compound-action snips with a piercing tip. This makes starts quicker and easier. Otherwise, in making a hole or opening in sheet metal, use a punch or chisel to create a hole in which the snips can be inserted.

NIPPERS. End-cutting nippers have blunt-nosed jaws which can cut bolts and rivets close to the surface. They will cut heavy wire and nails. They are for heavy cutting and twisting.

A special type of end-cutting nippers is used for cutting tile, especially small ceramic mosaics. When completely closed, the jaws are still about ⅛″ apart and, unlike those of ordinary nippers, are off-center.

10 | Prybars / Nailpullers

"Give me a lever and a place to stand, and I will move the world," said Archimedes, the Greek inventor who, over 2,000 years ago, understood the enormous power of this simple device. Today, the homeowner frequently needs the added muscle that leverage can give him. A nail that a hammer can't budge, a wrecking bar with its added leverage can extract with little effort. For prying apart boards, lifting heavy weights, dismantling a brick wall, laying stone, getting under a log, opening a wooden box or crate, and dozens more jobs, leverage tools are indispensable.

How do you pull out a sunken nailhead? With a nail claw. It's a sharp-edged claw at the end of a lever. With a hammer, pound the claw under the nailhead, then rock the lever back to lift the head. The claw end of these tools has varying degrees of curvature or offset. The curve or offset serves as a fulcrum.

Where space won't permit you to get in with an offset design, you can use a puller with an almost straight claw. After you have the nail started, you can slip a block of wood under the bar to act as a fulcrum. Nail pullers like these may be of hexagonal or round stock and 11" to 14" in overall length.

For pulling up old flooring boards or taking out a partition, a ripping chisel is the tool to use. Usually 18" long, with a ¾" hex shaft, it has dual nail slots. One is at the end, and is like a claw. The other, just back of it, is a teardrop opening which can be dropped over a nailhead. It is just the right distance from the end to give excellent leverage. You can pound with a hammer on the end of a ripping chisel's shaft if you have to. Millers Falls makes a ripping chisel with an offset at the pounding end. This provides a larger target for the hammer, as well as an extra claw puller. A bar similar to this one is made of lighter-weight flat steel.

A wrecking bar has one slightly offset chisel end, for prying. The other end has a gooseneck shape and is specially designed for pulling up tough nails and spikes. Most wrecking bars are 18" to 30" long.

Designed especially for wedging, and for cutting nails behind flooring or siding, the electrician's cutting chisel has a

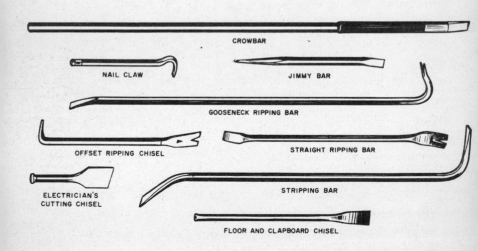

CROWBAR

NAIL CLAW

JIMMY BAR

GOOSENECK RIPPING BAR

OFFSET RIPPING CHISEL

STRAIGHT RIPPING BAR

ELECTRICIAN'S
CUTTING CHISEL

STRIPPING BAR

FLOOR AND CLAPBOARD CHISEL

broad flat blade. With a somewhat narrower blade and a longer shaft is the floor and clapboard chisel. As its name implies, its specialty is clapboard removal and attendant nail cutting. It's good for prying in depth.

A lining-up bar is designed for prying and aligning jobs. It is sometimes called a jimmy bar. This is a tool especially useful in metal work. The end with the long slim taper is for lining up bolt and rivet holes.

TOOL	PURPOSE	COMMON SIZE
Crowbar	Heavy-duty prying, lifting, wrecking, concrete breaking	4'
Gooseneck ripping bar	Wrecking, prying, heavy nail pulling	36"
Nail claw	Driving under sunken nailheads and pulling	11"
Jimmy bar	Close-quarter prying, nail pulling in close quarters	16"
Straight ripping bar	Wrecking, prying, nail pulling in close quarters	36"
Stripping bar	Removing forms from poured concrete, prying, lifting, wrecking	36"
Electrician's cutting chisel	Shearing tongues and nails in flooring, wedging	8"
Offset ripping chisel	Prying, driving under nailheads, 3-step pulling	18"
Floor and clapboard chisel	Removing clapboards, shearing nails, opening crates, prying	18"

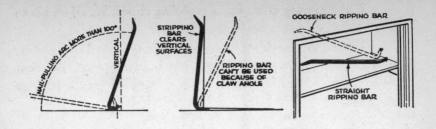

Gooseneck ripping bar (left) has tremendous leverage but needs a long swing. It's not good for starting nails—for that you need a nail claw. Because stripping bar (center) has a shallower hook than a gooseneck, it can get up close to vertical surfaces. Choose it for lifting a safe, refrigerator, or for prying up anything heavy. The flat claw of a straight ripping bar (right) lets you get in and pull nails a hammer couldn't reach. It can also get in where a gooseneck can't.

For moving rocks, boulders, and breaking up concrete, choose the crowbar. It is a straight bar, tapered at one end and usually 4' to 6' long. If your object is lifting you must provide your own fulcrum. For prying out a boulder, or wedging into a crack in a brick wall, it is unexcelled. Being straight, it offers better control than an angled bar.

For removing trim, use a molding chisel. Its offset blade is 2″ wide and has a beveled nail slot.

Every shop needs at least one cat's-paw type of nail puller. A gooseneck ripping bar comes next in importance. Between these two tools, you can do most jobs. Add the others later as need arises.

11

Tools for Measuring and Marking

A good part of the time on any project is spent measuring and marking. The right measuring equipment will help you to do the job faster and better.

MEASURING TOOLS.   Your first choice for most measuring jobs should be a metal tape. There are several points to watch in selecting one. Don't buy a 6′ tape. The first time you try to measure a 4-by-8 sheet of plywood or plasterboard, you'll wish you hadn't. Even an 8-footer is inconvenient for many jobs, but it does have the merit of being light in your pocket.

A 10′ rule is a good choice. Its tape is ½″ wide, and so it's still a compact package. A 12′ rule usually has a ¾″-wide tape, and so becomes considerably bulkier and heavier. If you're involved in a big project, like building an addition or adding a shed dormer, you will find a 12′ tape useful. You may like a 16′ tape even more. There are few measuring jobs it can't handle in a single take.

Whatever you do, get a tape that is marked both in inches and in feet-and-inches. If you get one marked in feet-and-inches only, you'll get involved in translating measurements

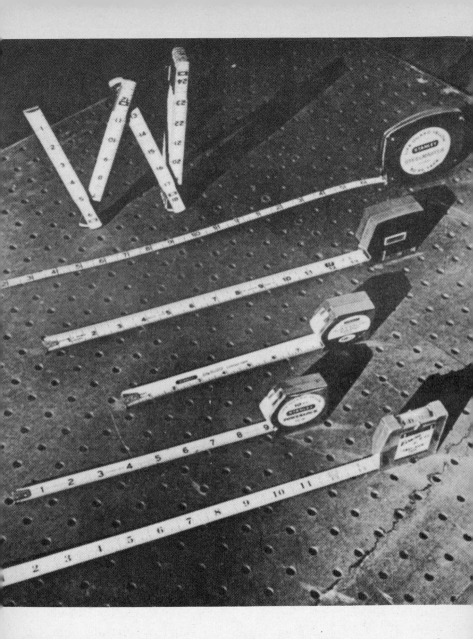

Metal tapes come in a variety of styles. A good choice is a
10′ tape marked in inches and feet-and-inches. Six-foot
folding rule at rear still has some adherents.

from inches to feet-and-inches, and who can do that success-fully for very long? Some tapes don't have a power return. You have to push them back into the case. This is a nuisance.

It's convenient to have at least two tapes. Then you can have one at your project site and another at your table saw. Most shops eventually collect a half-dozen tapes, but one or two are favorites and get almost all the use.

Wooden rules. Asked why he used a folding wood ruler when it was so much slower than a tape, a carpenter replied with a grin, *"That's* the idea."

A zigzag or folding rule is no more accurate than a push-pull rule. The push-pull rule is almost universally used in the cabinetmaking industry where accuracy is far more demand-ing than in carpentry. Cabinetmakers like it because it allows the measurement of both regular and irregular shapes as well as the taking of inside and outside measurements. Also popu-lar is the 24″ folding rule. It folds into a 6″ length, easy to tuck into a pocket. Often made of boxwood, it is now also available in white nylon which is impervious to moisture and humidity. Its hardware is stainless steel. Gradations are very distinct and easy to read.

Try square. The try square is a blade set into a handle at a 90-degree angle. It is a tool for marking lines at right angles across a board so you can get a true cut. You can use it to check corners and joints to see if they are exactly right-angled. You can also use it to check boards for warping and cupping. With the blade set across a board, any light visible beneath the blade as it is slid along will show exactly where the board is out of square.

Some try squares have a handle that makes a 45-degree miter where it meets the blade. These are sometimes called miter squares. By placing the handle's angle against the edge of a board, a 45-degree miter cut can be marked. Since a miter square does everything a try square does and marks miters besides, get it if you can.

Try square is essential for marking lumber for true cuts, and for checking right angles of corners and joints.

Steel or rafter square. A book could be written about the many uses of the steel square, and many books have been.

If you are building a roof, this is the square to use. Tables on the square will enable you to make all the rafter cuts and notches that would otherwise be almost impossible. But a steel square has many other uses besides roof-building.

The short, wide blade on a steel square is called the body. The long, narrower blade is called the tongue. Typically, the body measures 24″ by 2″ and the tongue 16″ by 1½″. Because of its large size, the steel square can do many layout jobs that are beyond the capabilities of a try square. Cabinetmakers use a steel square for marking the angles on a supporting brace, as well as determining its length. They use it instead of a protractor for laying out angles of varying degrees. If you're building a planter with sloping sides, a steel square can give the measuring information you need. Because of its size, it's

Steel square being used with screw-on gauges to mark repeated cuts on a stair stringer. Square is also used to measure and mark rafters, angles of braces, etc. Tables on the square give data for measuring rafters.

the best square to use for marking on plywood or other large surfaces.

Combination square. This is like a try square except that its handle can be slid to any point along the length of the blade. Because of the sliding handle, it can be used as a marking gauge and a depth gauge. Its handle or beam may include a level and a removable scriber. It makes a convenient plumb, level, and straightedge. The angle on its handle permits marking off 25-degree as well as 90-degree angles.

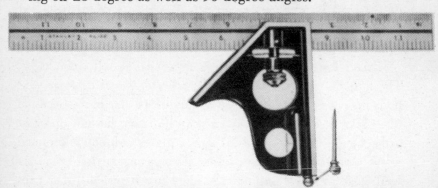

Combination square has a handle with 90- and 45-degree angles which slides along blade. Handle contains a bubble level and a metal scriber. Many uses of the tool are shown at right.

STRAIGHT EDGE

INSIDE TRY SQUARE

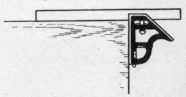

OUTSIDE TRY SQUARE

LEVEL

PLUMB

MARKING GAUGE

DEPTH GAUGE

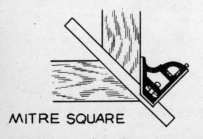

MITRE SQUARE

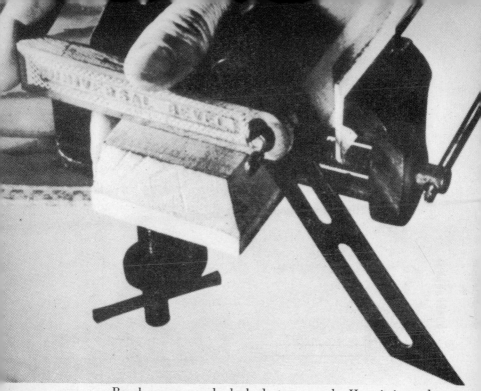

Bevel square can be locked at any angle. Here it is used to check a bevel being planed on both sides of a board.

One variant of the combination square has all the usual features plus these in addition: It can be used as a nail, screw, or dowel gauge. It can be used as a protractor and beam compass. It can be extended to 16″ for use as a stud marker.

Bevel square. The blade on this square can be set at any angle from 1 to 179 degrees and locked there by means of a thumbscrew. You can set it on work and adjust its blade to match the exact angle required for a perfect fit. The bevel square is sometimes called the sliding T bevel because it can be used to lay out and test the angle of a bevel.

ROUGH MEASURING. Mark off feet or inches on a post or Lally column in your shop. It's both useful and decorative.

Measure your stride. By adjusting your natural stride to make it either shorter or longer, you can learn to pace off distance in 2' intervals with good accuracy.

Measure the span of your hand. If it comes out exactly 9", you have a ready means of estimating whether a board is 8", 9", or 10" wide.

What is your reach with both arms extended? If it's exactly 6', you have it made.

Other good built-in measurements are the breadth of your hand, and the breadth of your hand with thumb extended. Most men find the former to be approximately 3" and the latter 7".

LEVELS. In this tool, a bubble in a glass tube or vial tells you when work is level or plumb, or how much it is off. You need levels not only for such jobs as setting fence posts vertical, shelves horizontal, and making a drain pipe pitch at exactly the right slope, but for every kind of construction job. Three basic levels belong in every well-equipped shop.

Aluminum level with six vials is used here to check work in progress on a ceiling. Center vials register for horizontal reading, end vials for vertical.

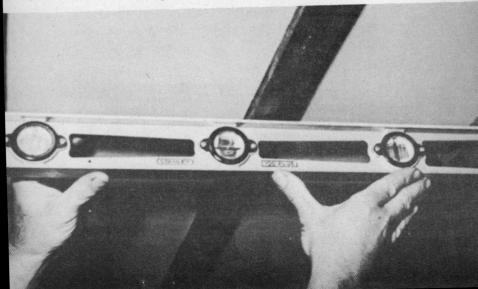

First, you need a 24″ aluminum-frame level. You'll use this for most jobs and it is important that it be accurate. A good level has six vials, so that no matter how you pick it up, it's always in the right position for taking a reading.

Check the accuracy of all vials before you buy. Here's how: Put it on any flat horizontal surface. If it doesn't register level, put some folded paper under one end until you get a level reading. Now reverse the level by swapping ends. The level's bubble should come to dead-center again. Check the plumb vials by the same swapping technique. If a level doesn't read the same in both directions, its calibration is off. Some levels have adjustable vials. This is some help in correcting inaccuracies, but adjustment requires considerable care.

When vials are paired, read the lower vial. If there is just one vial, be sure the vial is turned with its curved side up. When checking the horizontal, a bubble will move toward the high side of the level. In checking a vertical the bubble moves away from the direction in which the vertical tilts. Read the bubble carefully. If you are setting framing, or anything else that's vertical, and you doubt the accuracy of your reading, use a plumb bob as a check. A plumb bob is never wrong. For checking a horizontal, you can also use the plumb bob. Establish the true vertical, then get your horizontal by setting a rafter square blade against it.

You can't get into tight spots with a 2′ level. That's why a 9″ torpedo level is essential. If you think it gets its name from its shape, you're right. A typical torpedo level has three vials—horizontal, vertical, and 45-degree. A torpedo level can be a lifesaver, but don't use it unless you have to. Because of its small size, it's much more difficult to get an accurate reading.

The third level you need is a "line level," a single-vial device which hooks onto a line. It enables you to take a level reading over a considerable distance. For instance, you can use it for establishing the level of a fence, a garden wall, or a foundation. For an accurate reading, your line must be kept very taut. If your eye is sharp, you won't be more than ½″ off in 60′.

That much error isn't bad for many projects, but it isn't good enough for a house foundation. To come within ⅛″ of target in 80′ you can use a pair of inexpensive sights that clamp to a 2′ level. In use, the sight-equipped level is placed on a level table. The target is a 3″-by-5″ file card which an assistant slides up and down on a vertical rod. When the lineup is dead-center on the target, you've established the horizontal you are after. Reverse the level and take additional sightings to verify your accuracy.

If you undertake any masonry construction, you'll need a 4′ mason's level. It will bring an accuracy to your work that a 2′ level can't match.

MAKING YOUR MARK.   The thickness of a pencil line may be all that stands between you and perfect craftsmanship. A carpenter's broad-lead pencil is all right for marking 2-by-4s but for cabinet work you need something more pointed. Use either a very sharp pencil or a marking knife. A scratch-awl can be used for marking, though its main talent is for marking hole locations and for making starting holes for screws and brads.

To avoid measuring mistakes, cut a stick to the length you need. This is especially handy when you have many pieces to cut to the same length. A more elaborate version of a measuring stick is a technique known as "rod layout." Every measurement needed for the construction of a project, such as a cabinet, is made on a length of wood, such as a 1-by-2. This 1″-by-2″ "rod" must be longer than the longest-sized board that is required. Height, width, and depth measurements are each marked on a different side of the rod. You can then forget about using a ruler.

The easiest way to draw the line for a job like trimming

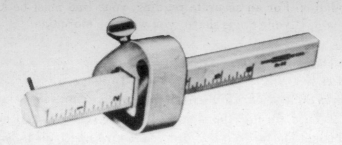

Marking gauge is used to scribe a true line along the edge of a board. It's more accurate than a pencil.

1″ off a board is with a *marking gauge*. This tool, usually of wood, has a head which slides on a beam that's just under 8″ long. By turning a thumbscrew you can fasten the head at any point along the beam. At the end of the beam there's a projecting spur. In use, the head is held firmly against the edge of the board and by pushing it away from you, the spur scores the required line.

Where extreme accuracy is not needed, you can improvise a marking gauge using a ruler, with your clenched hand as the sliding head. For example, if you want to make a mark 1″ from the edge of a board, hold a ruler so that 1″ of it projects onto the board. Place the point of the pencil at the end of the ruler and slide the ruler along the board's edge, making a mark as you go.

A *chalk line* (a length of twine impregnated with chalk dust) is the only means of marking a long line with accuracy. The line, resting on the surface, is pulled taut between the points where the mark is to be made. A few inches from one end, the line is picked up between thumb and forefinger and then released. As it snaps back, it deposits a line of chalk that is easy to follow.

Chalk lines are used in laying floor tile or shingles in a straight line. Some chalk lines come in containers that you can fill with white or blue chalkdust. You can also buy small hemi-

Chalk line makes a straight line on a large surface, useful in laying floor tiles or shingles. Here the line, after being snapped, is raised to show chalk mark.

Pair of dividers is used to scribe tiles and paneling to conform to irregularities in the wall line.

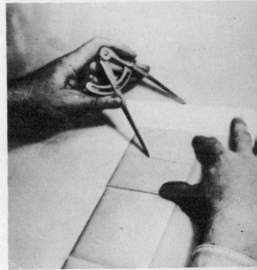

Contour gauge lets you "lift" complicated shapes so that they may be copied. Adjustable wires conform to any shape they're pressed against.

spheres of blue or white carpenter's chalk, and chalk any length of twine for the purpose.

Dividers and compasses have more use than just scribing small arcs and circles. They can be used for fitting a shelf, cabinet, or flooring against an uneven wall. With one leg held against the wall and drawn along it, the other leg will record every irregularity on material held against the wall.

Another good device for handling irregularities, especially such problems as fitting around moldings, is a *contour gauge*. Its adjustable wires can be fitted to any irregular surface and pick up its exact conformation.

12

Clamps and Vises

CLAMPS. Clamps are extra hands. Stronger than human hands, they give you the muscle to do many tasks you would otherwise find impossible. There are at least five of the following types that you'll find useful around the shop. Each has its own special purpose. A generous assortment will make many jobs easier and improve the quality of your work.

Adjustable hand screws. These clamps have wide wooden jaws so the chances of marring wood on which they are used are minimized. They can be used without protective pads under their jaws. They can be adjusted to clamp angular or irregular work. By turning only one screw, the jaws close at an angle instead of parallel to each other.

Hand screws are adjusted by holding the right hand on the end screw, and the left on the screw which goes through the middle of the jaws. Revolving the end screw in a clockwise direction closes the jaws. Revolving it in a counterclockwise direction opens them. Place the jaws on the work so that the jaw area near the center screw touches first. Then, when you pull the jaw tips up tight, you'll obtain maximum pressure.

C-clamps. One glance at these clamps and you'll know why they were so named. Primarily designed for metalworking, they have many uses including the clamping of wood.

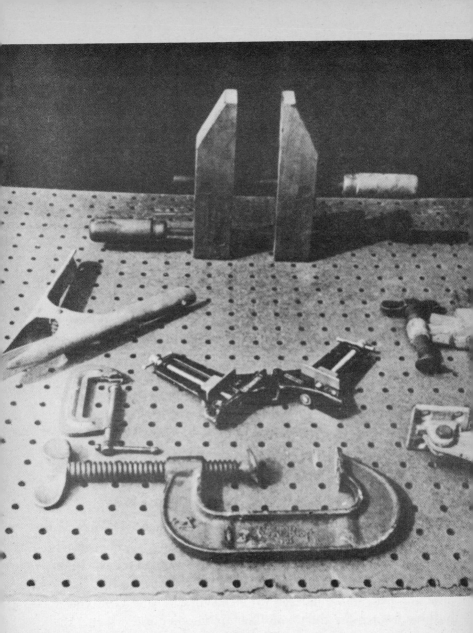

Some of the most useful clamps (from the top, clockwise):
hand screw; bar clamp; large and small C-clamps; spring
clamps. Miter clamp is at center.

When used on wood, it is usually necessary to use pads of scrap wood under their jaws to prevent marring the work.

You can get small, lightweight C-clamps whose maximum opening is 1″ and big, heavy iron ones that open 8″. Throat depth is limited in standard C-clamps, but there is one variety that has a throat depth two or three times that of standard clamps.

Bar clamps. Available in sizes ranging from 2′ to 8′, bar clamps are indispensable in making furniture and built-ins. They adjust by means of a movable jaw at one end and a crank that turns a screw at the other. Scrap wood pads must be used under their jaws to prevent marring. The pressure they exert is tremendous.

Pipe clamps work the same as bar clamps except that the jaws slide on pipe. You buy the set of jaws, supply your own length of ¾″ threaded pipe. Because you can use any length of pipe, this arrangement has great flexibility. It is also an economical way to get large clamps for spanning cabinet-sized dimensions.

Spring clamps. Resembling big clothespins, these handy items come in sizes that open from ½″ to 4″. Some come with plastic-covered tips to minimize marring the work.

Spring clamps do not hold as tightly, or exert as much pressure, as screw-type clamps, but their uses are legion. The larger sizes are generally more useful. It's a good idea to get at least four of each, but if you get a dozen you won't be sorry. They are quick and easy to use.

Corner or miter clamps. You need these for making screens, window sash, picture frames, or whenever you want to get a tight corner joint. Miter clamps will hold any degree of miter joint and prevent it from slipping. You can nail or screw the joint while the clamps are in place.

A typical set of four clamps will hold pieces up to 3″ in width and almost any length. They can be fastened to the workbench, if desired. However, there is one set that substitutes a

Three methods of storing clamps in the shop. Steel clamp hangers (top), made especially for the purpose, fasten to the walls with screws and support heavy loads. A board bracketed to the wall (center) serves as a storage rack. If joists are within reach, they make a good place to store long bar clamps (bottom).

"miter-box clamp" as the fourth clamp in the set. This accommodates a backsaw or handsaw, adjusting to blade width, and can be used as a guide in cutting a perfect 45-degree angle miter.

Also useful in holding miters firm are "pointed-end" clamps. These are applied by means of a plier-like spreader. They go on quickly and have heavy tension. A set of eight of these spring clamps, four of each of two sizes, along with a spreader, costs less than a set of standard corner clamps. They will handle stock from ⅝" to 1¾" in width. There is also a larger size with a capacity of 1¾" to 3½".

Band clamps. These use a fabric band for clamping around irregular-shaped work, like the four legs of a chair.

Bench holdfast. This is for clamping work firmly to the top of a workbench. It consists of a collar that sets flush into a hole bored in the bench top. The shaft of the holdfast fits into the collar. Turning a screw tightens an arm firmly down on the work. It has the maximum reach of 5⅞". Extra collars are available so that you can use the holdfast in more than one place.

Hinged clamps are available that attach to the underside of the front edge of your bench. In use, they swing up and a sliding head and screw hold the work firmly to the bench top. When not needed, the clamp swings under the bench.

Useful tricks with clamps. Have you ever had the experience of trying to clamp a series of boards in a bar clamp and have them buckle? You can use a hand screw to keep them in line. Place a board at right angles across the work you are clamping, and fix it in place with a hand screw. Now, no matter how tightly you turn the bar clamp, the work can't buckle.

Have you ever had a board that's too long and heavy to hold in a vise? Give the vise an assist by supporting the board at the other end of the bench with a hand screw clamped to the bench top.

Use two hand screws for holding a door when you are

planing its edge. Set the door on 2-by-4s near the front of the bench. Clamp one hand screw near the top edge of the door so that its flat side rests on the bench top. Use the second screw to clamp the first hand screw to the bench top.

When a badly cupped board won't fit into a dado, draw it up flat against a length of 2-by-4 using a clamp at the center of the bulge. The board will give you no further argument.

When you are trying to move something and there's nothing to get a hold on, use a C-clamp as an improvised handle. Just be sure you tighten it enough so that it won't pull loose.

Make a press for flattening records, or anything else that's warped out of shape, by using two sheets of ¾" plywood of appropriate size and a C-clamp on each side to hold the sandwich together.

Who will hold the other end of that heavy board when you have no helper? Clamp a cleat to a post, stud, rafter, or other support, and rest the board's end on it.

Use a clamp to fasten a stop lock or fence to the table of your saw to make a series of cutoffs of equal length.

For clamping two boards at right angles, such as when making a drawer, set a heavy-duty shelf bracket into the angle made by the two boards and use two C-clamps to hold the bracket in place.

When your largest clamp isn't large enough, use two clamps in tandem. Hook the end of one clamp inside the end of the other. You won't get a reach equal to the combined capacities of the two clamps, but you'll come near it.

SELECTING A VISE. The first choice for any shop is a *utility* or *bench vise*. It mounts on top of the bench and is designed for holding metal.

Big vises bolt to the bench top. Smaller ones may clamp on and have the advantage of portability, but they don't have the strength to handle all the jobs that come up in the average household.

104

Bench vise is essential in any shop. This one screws to the bench top, has a swivel base, pipe jaws below its main jaws, and anvil in rear.

Vises that bolt down may have a fixed base (usually the cheaper ones) or a swivel base. The latter may let the vise swivel a full 360 degrees, or 165 degrees—enough for ordinary purposes. There are kits available for converting stationary vises into the swivel kind.

Some vise jaws have serrated faces. These give the surest grip. But if you're finicky about preserving the finish of your work, you may be happier with smooth-faced jaws. If you have a vise with serrated jaws, you can get smooth caps to go over them, or you can improvise your own. Jaw faces may become worn after a while. Some vise manufacturers offer replaceable jaws. To prevent marring work, use a protective metal pad that is softer than your work. Brass is softer than steel, copper is softer than brass, and lead is softer than copper. The relatively narrow jaws of a bench vise can exert a pressure of many

All-angle bench vise mounts on a post and swivels 360 degrees. It can be used upright (left) or on its side (center). With a collar adapter, it can also tilt (right). Vise locks automatically in position as you tighten the jaws.

tons. If you're not careful, they can easily mangle many metals.

Some vises have pipe jaws below the regular jaws. If you don't own a pipe vise, this can be a handy feature. These curved, toothed jaws take a firm bite on many round objects that regular jaws can't handle effectively.

Woodworker's vise. This is the one other vise that every shop needs. The bench vise handles metal jobs, and this one handles wood. Unlike the bench vise, the woodworker's vise mounts below the bench, with its jaws flush with the bench top.

The best woodworker's vises have these two features: 1. A dog or stop in its outer jaw which can be raised above the bench level. This permits clamping work between it and the back of the bench or a bench stop. 2. Quick-acting jaws that open and close without laboriously screwing every inch of the way. The

Good woodworker's vise should have at least a 12″ capacity. Underbench mounting, an advantage of this model, keeps the top clear and work low for easy sawing and planing. Jaw can be slid in or out for fast setting; the screw engages only for final tightening against work.

Two-way carpenter's vise holds work either horizontally across the bench or vertically off the end. For portable use, it can be clamp-mounted to a sawhorse.

screwing is only for final adjustments.

There is a small clamp-on woodworker's vise that is handy as an auxiliary, or if you are not ready to make an investment in the kind that fastens on a bench permanently. This portable vise has L-shaped jaws which open to 2¾". They can hold work either horizontally across the bench or vertically at its end. Each jaw is 5½" long.

Vise advice. A vise can easily damage wood or metal. Always protect your work. A scrap block of wood, a sheet of cardboard or plastic, or a piece of sheet metal may be all it takes to save the day.

Apply only enough pressure, no more. Most vises are designed to take only as much pressure as you can apply on the handle with your own hands. If you slip a length of pipe over the handle for extra leverage, you may break the vise.

Once in a while, oil the moving parts on the vise. Wipe away the excess with a clean rag.